The Second-Violoncello Method

by
A.W. Benoy
and
L. Burrowes

NOVELLO

EXCLUSIVELY DISTRIBUTED BY
 HAL•LEONARD®

NOV915969

Lesson 1

Crossing Strings. Key C major

YE HOLY ANGELS BRIGHT

J. DARWALL

THE IRISH WASHERWOMAN

SONG from "PEASANT CANTATA"

J.S. BACH

CELLO 1

5

CELLO 2

Allegro moderato

Dal Segno ℅ al Fine **ff**

4

HIGHLAND SONG

BUNESSAN

Lesson 2

Fourth Position, first finger only

EXERCISES

Paxton

15969

CAPTAIN MORGAN'S MARCH

WELSH AIR

THE KEYS OF CANTERBURY

Paxton

NOW THANK WE ALL OUR GOD

J. CRÜGER

THE FROG AND THE MOUSE

Lesson 3

Fourth Position, Key G major

SCALE

12

ARPEGGIO

13

MUSETTE

G. F. HANDEL

Tranquillo

CELLO 1
14
CELLO 2
CELLO 3

p

dim. — — pp

Paxton

LAND OF MY FATHERS

IT WAS A LOVER AND HIS LASS

T. MORLEY

CELLO 1

16

CELLO 2

THE MERRY PEASANT

R. SCHUMANN

Lesson 4

Fourth Position, Key C major

MOSCOW

F. GIARDINI

PEACEFUL SLUMBERING OCEAN

S. STORACE

THE SHOEMAKER

ANDANTE FROM STRING QUARTET IN A MINOR, Op. 29

F. SCHUBERT

22

Lesson 5
Half Position

EXERCISES

23

a Allegro

b Andante

c Con moto

AIR

H. PURCELL

Moderato

CELLO 1

24

CELLO 2

p (2nd time pp)

PRINCE RUPERT'S MARCH

DOWN AMONG THE DEAD MEN

IT IS ENOUGH

F. MENDELSSOHN

Lesson 6

First finger extended backwards. Key B♭ major

SCALE

28

(a) Separate bowing, one note to a bow. (b) Slurred bowing, two crotchets to a bow.

ARPEGGIO

29

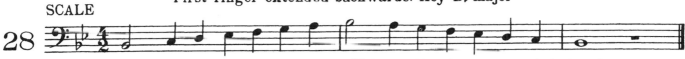

(a) Separate bowing. (b) Slurred bowing, four crotchets to a bow.

CZECH FOLK SONG

CELLO 1

30

CELLO 2

FARANDOLE

BIZET

WELSH AIR

PASSION CHORALE

J. S. BACH

Lesson 7

First finger extended backwards. Key F major

ARPEGGIO

34

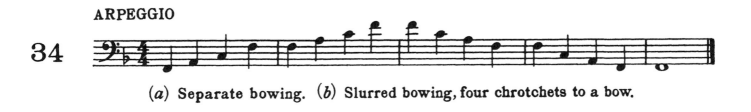

(a) Separate bowing. (b) Slurred bowing, four chrotchets to a bow.

EXERCISE

Andante

35

Paxton

15969

GATHERING PEASCODS

Paxton

15969

D.C. al Fine

CONTENTMENT

W. A. MOZART

Grazioso

CELLO 1

37

CELLO 2

A STRONGHOLD SURE

M. LUTHER

SING, LAUGH AND BE MERRY

H. G. NAGELI

Lesson 8

Forward finger extension. Key A major

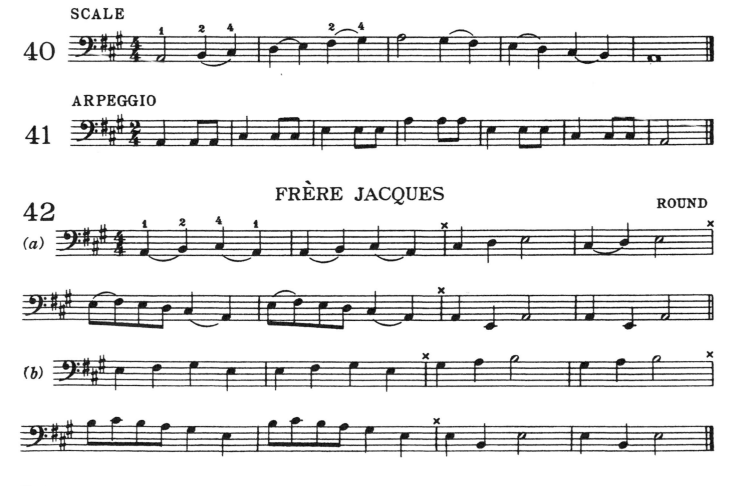

ST. THEODULPH

M. TESCHNER

THE SNOWY-BREASTED PEARL

LE PETIT RIEN

F. COUPERIN

Lesson 9

Forward finger extension. Key D major

SCALE

46

(a) Separate bowing. (b) Slurred bowing, two crotchets to a bow.

Paxton   15969

ARPEGGIO

47

WELSH HERO'S SONG

48

AUSTRIAN HYMN

J. HAYDN

Adagio

CELLO 1

49

CELLO 2

LAMENT FOR IRELAND

50 Con moto

THE KEEL ROW

Allegro non troppo

CELLO 1

51

CELLO 2
CELLO 3

Paxton

D. C. al Fine twice, *f, ff*

Lesson 10
Second Position

EXERCISES

LAVENDER'S BLUE

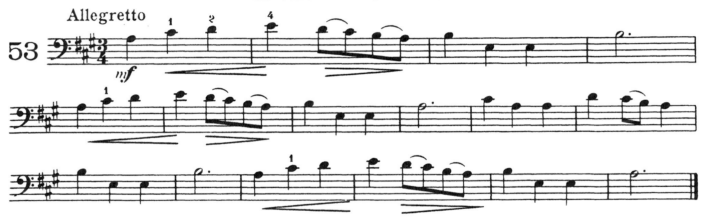

TRUMPET TUNE

H. PURCELL

IV Pos.

ff

allargando

tr

THE RISING OF THE LARK

Moderato

CELLO 1

55

CELLO 2
CELLO 3

mf (2nd time p)

mf

f

SONG OF THE WESTERN MEN

Lesson 11
Third Position

SCALE

(a) Separate bowing, one note to a bow (b) Slurred bowing, two crotchets to a bow

EXERCISE
Deciso

PROVENÇAL SONG

15969

RAKES OF MALLOW

CHORALE

J. S. BACH

EXERCISE

NOS GALAN

OVER THE MOUNTAINS

Lesson 12

Third Position

EXERCISE

65

TRADITIONAL RHYME

66

FLOWERS OF THE FOREST

COME LET'S BE MERRY

EXERCISE

EXERCISE

THEME

W. A. MOZART

ECOSSAISE

L. van BEETHOVEN

D. C. al Fine

The Second-Year Cello Method

Order No: NOV 915969

12 lessons covering crossing strings in key of C major, fourth position in keys of G & C major, half position, first finger extensions backwards in keys of Bb & F major, forward finger extensions in keys of A & D major, second position, and third position.

ALSO AVAILABLE SEPARATELY

The First-Year Cello Method

Order No: NOV 915905

15 lessons covering open strings and first finger notes, first and second finger notes on D & A strings, bowing on successive open strings, first and third finger notes on G, D & A strings, bowing with two notes to the bow, and scales of G, D & C major.

The Third-Year Cello Method

Order No: NOV 916111

10 lessons covering harmonics on A & D strings, tenor clef, fifth position, sixth position, seventh position, thumb position and treble clef, and higher positions.